The Phoenix Living Poets

CAIRNS

The Phoenix Living Poets

★

CAIRNS

by

CHRISTOPHER
LEVENSON

CHATTO AND WINDUS

THE HOGARTH PRESS

1969

Published by
Chatto and Windus Ltd
with The Hogarth Press Ltd
42 William IV Street
London W.C.2
★
Clarke, Irwin and Co Ltd
Toronto

SBN 7011 1486 X

Printed in Great Britain by
William Lewis (Printers) Ltd Cardiff

For My Father

ACKNOWLEDGMENT

Some of the poems here were first published in the following magazines and anthologies:

Ambit, Arena (USA), Best Poems of 1966, Commonwealth Poets of Today, Critical Quarterly, Delta, English, English Poetry Now, The Listener, London Magazine, The Manoeuvering Sun, Midland – 2, New Campus Writing – 7, New Poems – 1965, New Statesman, North American Review, North East (USA), Outposts, Poetry Magazine (Australia), Poetry Northwest (USA), Poetry 1960, South and West (USA), Spectator, Texas Quarterly, Transatlantic Review, Unicorn, Universities Poetry – 4.

Two were read on the BBC programme "The Poet's Voice", several on the University of Iowa radio station WSUI, and one on TWW television.

Contents

The Birth

At whitest intensity the blank walls reject
Her cries. All night, facing this birth alone,
She carried her burden, and despite
The calm sister-shrouds that attended her, the white-smocked
    doctors,
When she asked deliverance from her bearing down,
Nothing we said
Could penetrate that circle where her child
Attracted all feeling to its burning core, anaesthetized
All sound into icy silence.

So dry words will not kindle, nor the clay set,
Until in silence all has been worked out, finally through
    pain
Exorcised, and lies there on the sheet, a separate being.
Then can the world flood back
And in that clay and in that burning, life.

Empty Rooms

When two years later my brother died there was no new
    growth
To seal the wound; her belly, clenched with pain
And ingrowing bitterness, did not heal
Around its now final emptiness. In vain she tried
New jobs, new countries, 'freedom' from home, from the past.
Becoming soured and vindictive, her words stripped the
    wallpaper
Of twenty years marriage, showed cracks the blitz had made,
Then went on steadily removing the lino,
Wrenching up floorboards, till they both saw
What rough and ready joists, sockets and wires
Held their jerry-built lives together, what gross draughts
They still suffered to whimper under the door.
Years she sat there, tight-lipped, statued in anger,
Then quit, leaving no address.

Now there is peace at last for the garden and books,
But the tools all rust, the flowers run to seed,
The house has filled with silence like a gas,
And each night in the faded drawing-room
My father, slippered, by the electric fire,
Sits alone, falling asleep over his book.

Cairns

— for Sylvia Plath —

Her death smiled from the paper
forewarning of distant landslides.
Something crumbles inside me, once more
the slowly established lines of communication
are left dangling above the wreck,
the patiently built encampments in the foothills
are blotted out, months, years wasted, a voice
lost in the snow.
As the search is called off lethargy
shadows the survivors like a mist.
All words are called in question, all heroic
vigour, movement, daring, all she was . . .
Though words fail us stones shall not
and in the mist her stony words shall serve
as cairns.

The only way with death is to take it daily
in small doses with your morning paper.
Gloat over earthquakes, fires,
tiny figures leaping from sinking liners.
Make your nerves taut, harden them to disaster.
But even then, suddenly, in bad weather,
some virus may intrude to strike you down.
For a moment the city stalls, reels, giddily
you clutch at railings, steady yourself, smile
at the absurdity of loss; then, losing momentum,
like the slipped carriages of an express
trundling to a halt in a country siding,
your world runs slowly down. Grass will in time
stifle this bright steel. But for now, for now
there is no cure, and nothing to say
that has not time and again already been said —
in vain.

The voice of a dead woman
reads her own poems over the radio —
presentiments, omens,
a shape on the horizon only she knew,
a burden, a growth, long carried within her
her poems now have exorcised. She lies
still-dead. We crowd with horror
the cast of the mind we had just begun to know
and find how little we knew.
We the survivors are accused by her death
of ignorance, in all our press, of pain.
The pollarded trees brandish their crutches for pity:
we do not see.
The factory sirens scream as they disgorge
their human fodder. We nod and pass by.
Ships in the estuary wail for the drowned:
we say, 'There's a gale blowing.'

Slowly eroded by successive deaths,
the foreland of my youth slips into the sea
in a whirlpool of mud, a high wave then, settling,
the same water,
the same element that when the dam burst drowned
thousands, yet left me dry-eyed
though in newsreels they angled dead men out of the trees.
Numbers bludgeon, we ignore the one.
At the slow onset of a fatal sickness
the extremities refuse to feel pain,
imagination's clogged, the heart wrung dry, I dread
my own impassivity.

Kind Sister Death has drawn a screen
about what was or might have been,
but we are marked and make our own
fragments of the life that's gone.
As when the barricades are down
looters invade the flooded town,

Among vacated flesh and blood
we leech for intellectual food.

A burning farm as we drove by
blazoned despair through the night sky:
fine images of terror and hate
distance will accommodate
or verse redeem; but walled in pain
all mortal wisdom proves in vain.
However love clamp bone to bone
we live apart, we die alone.
Those that survive need at most breath
to mourn an individual death.
Only the single grief is real
and the worst death is not to feel.

Dead Letters

How long had they waited there, accumulating dust,
These words written in fever, later forwarded
To an address where strangers had moved in
And sent back marked 'Unknown'?
Two sensible people, they realized
Love such as theirs could hardly hope to survive
The winter of their marriages and children.
Yet the attempt was made. At Christmas and New Year
They read between the lines and into the lines
All they would rather have said had they lain together.
Instead good wishes, useless as a single glove,
Cluttered the mantelpiece.

                         Hope had become mere habit
Long before death procured their separation.
His letter came too late,
Like the tapping of rescuers in the flooded mine
Or a telephone ringing in an empty room.

The Wall

When movement was still free between these zones
They met each evening, unobserved and silent,
In parks or cafes, plotting dangerous futures,
Their hands, their lips, their bodies wholly linked
In impossible union.

Then it became more difficult: a wall was built,
Sentries were installed between heart and hand,
Arc-lamps exploded the night and no special permits
Were issued to lovers. In their letters at first
They swore they would never forget, and were always
        planning
Tunnels, escape routes.

But one Sunday their white waving handkerchiefs fluttered
        surrender.
They walked away home along the sodden tramlines,
Each pretending the other did not exist,
That this was the whole world;
And life grew simpler, less life-like.

X-Ray

That is not knowing, seeing
through flesh to the vertebrae,
going beyond what is needed:
raw anatomies
cannot build home
here in this dark patch, that hollow
wound where love enters, — or would
if only these framed skeletons
could act.

Nothing to hold on to,
our own flesh and blood —
tissues, fabrications —
dissolves before our eyes
to splashes of light, shadow.
Machines record but who shall interpret
these phantoms, bone-locked?

Let the half-truths suffice.
Such excess knowledge
leaves nothing to explore.
I lie in wait for
your touching, knowing hands,
the tact that guides them,
the mystery they share.

Generations

To them I am already an old man. In this forcinghouse —
Vast walls of glass, corridors, classrooms, stairs
In half a dozen jarring pastel shades —
Their grasping minds reach out, their slender thighs,
Cramped into desks and benches, are held back
From flagrant blossoming, but their eyes
See past me, into other corridors.
We do not communicate. What can I say? The years,
So few, have grown between.
War, that is their mythology, was my youth,
And 'the one thing needful', experience, I cannot convey.

Fearing lest I become
Mere staid admonisher, I often read my 'change'
In the barometer of these teen-age faces,
Watch them through a mask of authority,
Hoping that girl does not guess how I recognize
In eyes, cheeks, hair, gesture and accent, another
Girl dead now, or that tall dreamy lad
Turn from his work to interpret my curious stare.
Too young for nostalgia, I will not overhear
Their brittle, bitter secrets, try not to see
What I in retrospect could have been, but fear,
Watching them learn so avidly, how paint and easy smile
Will soon disguise the child within. I learn to hide
My disappointments, my premonitions.
They too will know in time, too late,
The routine of growing old. Why tell them
Of flickering horizons they may never visit?
Tired, as they are, of my own voice talking,
I have nothing to say but 'Carry on reading, quietly.'

Things

I watch in despair
The house growing,
Things acquiring
An air of permanence,
Furniture that clings
To the bare makeshift walls;
Each way I turn, the bric-a-brac
Solid now and reliable
Hems in the past, seals off
All possible futures.
Souvenirs have become
Our permanent setting
Till like habitués
Of musty waiting rooms
We outstare the gay posters,
Acclimatize to the dust,
Aware that the one solution –
Leaving – is long past,
We have become the décor.

The Idealist

Heaven is other places, not here
And now, but last year's cloistered calm
At the foot of the Pyrennees, overgrown
By last summer's flowers.

Heaven is other people; here everyone
So cool and condescending, no real
Friends, only acquaintance; no soul's
Communion — chit-chat.

Crazy with discontent, her mind
Drills to detect
Inviolate gushing wells
Of kindred feeling that intellect,

Set on more precious stone, cannot cry down.
We are panned, sifted, discarded
As she prospects for the ideal, afraid
One day she may find it.

The Hospital

The day they let me go,
bathed, scoured and scrubbed dry,
I walked in a hospital
dressing-gown through the permanent
blue early dawn, a maze
of harsh windows all lit up
like the face of a child my own
age, lying swaddled
propped in white
bandages against red blankets.
Diphtheria, they told me.

The wards possess the whole night. Sister,
Sister, voices stifled by sleeping
alone call through red-lit corridors,
cry down the half-heard earphone music.
A sterile nurse stoops to admire
her pinned-back blonde hair in the silver
bedpan flusher, then slices wafer-thin
bread to be thinly buttered. Everything
is under control. The visitors have left
their debris of gifts, spent
children, and now like a barrage of light
the sleepless hospital
contests, holds back the darkness.

An Old Man Dying of Cancer

A voice inside him asks for a little soup:
That voice has taken everything. Stifled in rugs,
Scornfully he watches us feast at the piled table,
Keeping himself alive with hope and drugs.

Brisk, trilby-hatted in the photographs
Of two years back, but what can now disguise
The meaning of the scribbled hieroglyphs
In sunken cheek and hollow guarded eyes?

He knows why these enquiring relatives come
To wait on him. Forced to a hard bargain,
He has put aside vanity, quietly accepted his doom.
A knife of pain unstitches that self-made man.

The room is over-furnished for such ascetic grace.
Hand raised like a pope's gravely asserting
His last will, smiling, he staves off our embrace,
Sorry to embarrass us with his parting.

The Death of Shelley

' "Then what is life?", I cried' . . . And the sea answered.
As once before, caught unawares by storm
Off Meillerie, Shelley had merely sat and waited to drown,
So now, forcing daylight under, the thunderclouds suddenly
Break over the bay. A hasty shifting of sail,
Ropes slackened, the trim swift yachts
Race through taut waves to the quay, fasten alongside,
Wait for foul weather to pass. Only next day
Did the friends guess, the women questioning, and he,
How many leagues away, thinking perhaps
(For who knows if he tried to swim?) of his daughter
Whom he had last seen rising from the tide,
Found, as his mind's eye blinked, life's door slammed to.
On what unknown shore had his yacht run aground,
Leaving no trace? Who brought him lying there,
Hair uncorroded by the leaden sea
That three days coffined him?
Fragile daylight lay wrecked on this quiet shore
As behind sealed eyes he woke to his private death.
We who ponder the body, friends to the god,
Can find no solace in the rising sea
That shall drown us also. We did not believe he could die.
These are the living waters, these swiftly veering
Currents, changeable, not easily charted. Though we may a
        while
Let the tides ferry us, then haul, manhandle the sail
Till the sea-faring gulls dwindle and the yawl
Is spun all ways by ocean and wind, free on its own
Sure keel, even that is not freedom: there is none
But the knowledge of those who survive
To kindle the funeral pyre, to sound the bell,
To find that the heart will not burn, nor the stars vanish.

Three Minutes on Poetry

The microphone bobs towards me like a float.
At the other end of the rod in a swivel seat
The cameraman plays me, I am netted by lamps
And, cooped like a battery hen, I lay the answers
To two questions a minute.
'Our poet friend' I heard the technician call me,
The tame eccentric brought here this evening to sing for us
Like a pet canary. Cross-legged I try to relax
In my few yards of decor, cramped between
Hit songs and a feature on holidays.
The interviewer smiles, 'Now, tell me, Mr. Levenson . . . '
The well-rounded phrases fur my tongue like sloes
As we talk to nobody
But four flickering images of ourselves
Suspended across the studio, and catch ourselves smiling
Yes, nodding yes, for half a minute too long
After the sound was cut. A poet's job, I said,
Is to be concise. They had taken me at my word,
Having done their bit for culture for today.

At the Tombs of Keats and Shelley

Four minutes to closing time, I stand
at the English Cemetery in Rome,
uncertain of my homage,
taking a quick look.

And liking the place for its well-kept shade,
I confront these simple stones,
no less unacknowledged:
no ghosts rise to bid me welcome.

Damn the poetic dead:
greedy for fame, they took
the very words from our mouths
and crammed them into their own
along with the leafmould
of smouldering libraries.

Now they, first come, are stuffed full.
Emptily, I turn
and listen to my footsteps echo back
through residential glooms,
street names like epitaphs.

Fossil

Unviable, obdurate, recalcitrant,
rock strata yield
slowly at first
to nails, chisels,
driven hard in;

then as veins fracture, hands
break in upon
ramified lithic darkness,
lenses and fingers probe
some strange crustacean, pent
in its brittle shell
across millennia.
Who could have guessed
this unique, secret order,
scrambled, ghosted through stone?
We prize
the given shape,

making ourselves from this
enduring struggle
to become one with earth.

Statues

(Homage to Bosnia)

The scab of custom
Has crusted over the blood
And memory, running dry, dribbles out
In the sour mountain August
Where buried parents and sons
And what they died for
Are petrified on the dust-blown market square
In facile masks, their courage
Resurrected in statues.

Four years of agony
Redeeming four hundred,
This people locked in by mountains
Saw through a break in the cloud
A path straining upwards to the next valley.
Their deaths gave birth to a dream
That noonday consolidates
Elsewhere, in distant cities.
War's vultures picked
These villages clean as bone
And the rotting orchards of peace
Are how many days' journey
Over the parched mud?
Whilst here to endure the old ways,
To rest in the statues' shade
Bartering paprikas, piled high
Over cartwheels of solid wood,
Still needs courage enough.

Our Beloved Leader

When our beloved leader drove to his country villa
And his car collapsed miles from the nearest garage
He ordered new motor highways.
When even he succumbed to the typhus epidemic
He set up an Inquiry Commission to probe the sewers.
When he saw how few people could read his books and
      speeches
He outlawed illiteracy.

When he died a detachment of military gentlemen,
Intent only on preserving order
And mindful of his many services,
Erected a sixty foot statue to him,
To be paid for voluntarily
From the people's taxes.

For a Successful Revolutionary

My sympathies, Comrade!
The personality you cultivated now cut
down to size or less, encased in
a dozen grey suits, high office, a shiny car,
it is you who will wither away,
finding the slogans you invented
obsolete, the guns you used
stacked in museums, your speeches
out of print, and worst of all
the revolutionary spirit going flat.
Each year at the reunion
champagne explodes more hollowly.

That winter in the forest, '44,
those you left behind,
your truest comrades, the dead,
they would not have betrayed the ideal, but known
in their blood what words the new generations
would listen to, lost in their own way.
How few can still relive your sufferings!
The young say they are weary of heroics:
forgive them, they know no better, never knew worse.

Then it could have been different, then nothing
was settled; among the pines
plans whirled like snow.
Always on the move, the few survivors
with frostbite, amputations from the shoulder,
squatted in bivouacs each night planning
campaigns for their land's summer. Now
the peasants who fed you, smuggled messages, gave all
they had, grown old and prosperous,
hardly recognize their saviours.

State Visit

The children wait eagerly, or yawn, or cry.
A carriage clatters past. They wave; a hand
Waves back. Wagging their paper flags they stand
Bewildered by its golden brevity.

Being too young to remember when or why
We fought our guests, they simply take on trust
That honour is compact of blood and dust,
That for such glory men were made to die.

Death does not touch them, nor dare they disturb
The pensioner, as after the procession
He dreams old conquests back, but swerve to shun
The war-disabled beggar at the kerb.

Dust

Dust from the bomb sites, where the children exploring
Their new Pompeii as the morning sky
Is ripped open by jets, settles. The warning is unheard,
The sky is sealed again. Among the nettles
With sticks and rubber guns the children play.

Over the disused shelter a blackbird
Radiates fond certainty, and for the nature lover
Beauty is after all supreme. His music has weathered
So much catastrophe, why should we now imagine
Such urgent song augurs the long night in?

Why should we now imagine? Cement on the building sites
Is still indisputably solid, the world we built on stone
Shows no sign of falling, the rivers flow between concrete
And rows of stunted trees cut back too soon.
Only the microscope's eye sees in slow motion
The rotting marrow unthread the skeleton.

What can we do but warn? It is not war
That will murder our unborn heirs nor governments
That cloud their helpless future. Partly the terror
Decays us, mainly the dust, ceaseless and silent,
That chokes the fresh springs, seals the redundant treaties,
        slowly
Annihilates a world by accident.

Omens

Taking short cuts through the idle morning park
Where night is diluting slowly into dawn,
Its bleak light shaling the waters, I walk on
Through the collage of leaf-mould, bus-tickets, newspapers
That silts the deserted bandstand, while my sharp heels
Disinter skeletons, uneasy reminders
Of last summer's affluence.

                        When did autumn begin?
And when the winter? the first frost? the one decisive
Gale that assaulted the flaunting, golden trees
And stripped them of medals, showed their weals, their cancer?
Such dates find no place in diaries but are indelible.
Where only last week heavy winds fluted the lake
And residual outcrops of winter, dirty snow,
Gave no sign of daffodils, harsh rain sleeked the tarmac,
Trees flinched and cowered, spring was held
In abeyance, now this precious,
Precarious fashioning awakes to a sudden crowding of leaf,
The swept sky bleached and serene, overcome with blossom,
And everywhere brilliant tenderness, the grass lush
With clumps of lovers sprouting at every vista
And all the clandestine growth of crocus-lip or lilac
Thrusting into the open. All's bland assurance now.

But why such welcome? Why this perpetual
Flurry of acclamation? The half-built skyscrapers
Rock at their moorings, bitter sediments
Drift from the trees, brushing the ground like pollen.
When the routine streets are drowsy with sudden warmth
We forget the moles that tunnelled those placid lawns,
The stealthy rodents that gnaw distorted roots
Until the boughs creak, the trees fall, and the mind
Resigns itself to ruin, the accumulated terror.
This day, taken for granted, this confident green
May not be granted long — a glade reclaimed
From some lost childhood, sharp in scent and colour,

31

A definite event, pinned, painlessly killed
Like butterflies encased in sudden brilliance.

Not for the millions dead
Do I resent this disconcerting calm
Spring tricks us into accepting, but for the one
Small child at the lake's edge, playing unawares,
For the single grafted love that grows stunted or not at all,
A brief smile, a cadence of hair, now irrevocable
Before words could recall them. Why must these perish?

Mein Kampf

Almost diaphanous,
these slow-motion inmates lurch like drunks.
Almost shadow,
faltering, crushed by the sunlight's
sudden exposure,
or falling,
their legs crutches;
they patrol the frontiers of their walled no-man's-land,
will soon discard the last thin wraps of skin
for more substantial coverings.

Rather the puppets, rag dolls
grossly lolling, strings relaxed,
liberated by death,
than these still tenuously living
affronts to belief who insist on moving,
flickering black and white across the screen.
And this was victory, to release
imagination's ultimate? our flesh?

Once seen,
they do not die but in the sickened
breed the unthinkable, make it familiar.
They were not real before we smelt them, touched them,
felt them more human than we
who by our timely arrival suffered them
to go on living.

When will their images finally corrode
into what solution
stronger than love or pity?

Transit Camp

Quintessences of summer. Light breezes titillate
The terrace cafes where pink-faced stilted women,
Stiletto-heeled, pelican over their mocha.
Forks stab cream puffs, two well-trimmed poodles dance
Attendance, jacketted, begging for titbits. Swallows flirt
Among the striped awnings of the Opernplatz,
Our 'display window.'
                          A mile away
The wounds of amputation are staunched with cobwebs.
Flung up in the backwash of retreating armies,
The aged cling like barnacles to the blank walls
Of barracks, their nameless lives
Mortgaged to past and future, doubly outcast.
They came here in transit, would not learn the language
Their children gabble, had not meant to stay,
But, gradually drained of will, subsided into
The institutional grey. The spools of their minds
Wind backwards, summon flickering images,
All music and dialogue stopped.

The passage of time is a passage without turnings,
A dark corridor crammed with discarded wardrobes,
Light only at either end and that light grey.
The hope they read in the morse of sunset windows
They will not live to grasp. In unclaimed no-man's-lands
Their war continues, and with the soured persistence
Of weeds thrusting through cinder, flourishing
Radical discontent, they somehow survive, warnings.

War breeds a barren justice all its own:
How better could one have used decaying barracks?

34

Incognito

At the time it was only a name, an untidy sprawl
Of shading on a gridded and numbered map.
Red and black lines of road and railway converged,
Led, past the docks, to strategic factories.
These were the natural targets but the centre also
Had to be flattened — churches, schools, everything.

Our raid went according to plan — no flak and the night clear.
We unleashed our bombs and took our photographs
And, turning back, watched how railway tracks were
    embroidered
With tiny threads of fire as the flares sped down
Then flowered into majesty as the explosions swelled
Like salvos of jubilant fireworks, except for the sirens'
Wailing and the nagging sense that something was out of
    control.
Vast patterns of golden flame fanned out on the hillside,
Chased in wreathes of smoke. A few seconds sufficed
And the 'mission' was fulfilled, a thousand years' building
Razed like untimely sunset discoloured the night.

Later the newsreels displayed
Timbered houses cascading into the alleys,
Basements alive with children, a burning man
Leaps from the parapet, and in the city centre
Nothing left standing except where baroque facades
Stone Venuses, arose from a sea of rubble
(As the city itself in the undisturbed countryside)
Strange shells of dereliction. The radio
Reported our feat, giving data of dead and homeless.

I could not be there with the tanks as white dusters fluttered
Surrender from the ruins, nor join with the rescue squads
That rooted among the debris to disturb rags
And salvage what had been bodies;

Nor ever meant to visit the place — what was there to see? —
But one summer came by chance, changing trains
With half a night to spend there.

                                        And found her waiting.
That night her father, a chaplain, by an act of God
Had died and her brother, on home leave, was maimed for life
And hovered now in the ante-room, a cripple,
While we made love. Also her elder sister,
Loose-limbed and gay as a young tree, nursing
In one of the army hospitals and due
To marry a week later, was felled with one blow
Of the crumbling wall; and the books in the study were burnt
Through no fanatic zeal but because books
That enflame easily eagerly caught light,
Could not resist the wind.
So no-one remained but her and she was scared
Half out of her wits when the neighbours found her.
I felt her wound, a white patch on the thigh,
Inspected the black-framed photographs, glimpsed the cross
Discarded in one corner, saw on the mantelpiece
Fresh flowers to sweeten the dead, now celebrating
Their tenth birthday in her memory, alone
Of all who knew them.

                                        Until I had told her all
Her eyes seemed to sweep like dragnets through the lakes
Of my despondency, until she knew all I had
No leave to love but lay there cramped in fear.
I had never imagined myself so vulnerable.
I had never imagined.
So casually sown in a pavement cafe,
My longing, or love, took root, grew out of hand
And craved now not body only but absolution.

But when she knew, it was too late for anger
Or anything but regret. She smiled, tried to tell me
It was not I who killed, but the dials, the instruments,

36

Commanders in distant chart rooms, always the others.
But was not I too 'the other', the abstract enemy
Who now saw war embodied
In the blue channels of her veins and the red flow
Of blood through her heightened pulse as she lay there
Like an abandoned city? Only now, wondering
The contours of her limbs, could I guess what suffering
Lay folded in those maps and see how childhoods
Were broken by my half-conscious act, and sense
The grief films could not show me, the secret hopes
Buried beneath the mountains of that death.
So love created Europe in my heart
And grew discovery again, and hope, and fear,
Making an open city of our bed.

Keep Out!

Even so long after,
the mind's eye dilates
when at five works' sirens howl;
as dusk and the whole red sky
silhouette winding gear,
memory's thrown to the winds
like seed, like ashes.

Those crawling columns of lights
on the by-pass are only cars
returning home at rush hour;
and beyond, where the camp was,
more villas are shelved
against the smart hillside.

But no-one will tell you where
the last soldier died.
No presences from past wars
invade these resting woods,
no childhoods of barbed wire
can return here to weep.

Brambles annexed the bunkers,
soft, blurring weeds reclaimed
their place from concrete
till no joints or fists show through
their tight green skin.
An ailing wind still prowls
the emptied nissens, sometimes
chews at a bone or
in sudden fury unfurls
scraps of white paper, impaled
on a broken fence.
But no-one comes to read
such closely guarded secrets
and by nightfall
the wind too will have died.

Iceland

Ice-blue your eyes;
the sky pales after snow,
here we are secure.

But beyond those headlands
who knows
what treacherous currents,

what shoals of ice,
shock-latent, pack,
maraud

the crowded havens.
Red barns, stone walls,
wind-hung fields sown with rock,

the chandler's shack by the jetty,
await in glacial calm
twice weekly the white steamer;

its screws churn tidal waves
to dislodge crabs, bloat seaweed
and scrawl through misty water

a message for the gulls,
runes no-one can decipher —
versions of farewell?

Hammerfest

In harsh sunlight at five,
a windless dawn,
the first boats
dock. Small derricks
hoist bales, kegs,
fishing tackle.

Blurred by no trees,
toy blocks, the wooden houses,
reflect all colours
on the bay's still water
wherever rock allowed
a few yards of foundation.

Light only half the year,
a mere subsistence
eked out from fish
dried in the tarred
shacks by the jetty;
smoke ferries their stink

with the salt spray they rose from
above the seagulls' screams,
like a voice
from the other side,
islands hardly made out
except as a trick of light.

They seem content to watch
the fjord, long drawn out
into the dusk and the shale
sea pounding, chafing
the wharf and the silver
fish haul swung high
onto the quay.

The squat houses burn;
only the rocks
have security of tenure.
But those who inhabit them
also survive, worn down,
old faces dried like lichen.

New Building

Beyond the bridge a skeleton
blue-prints the sky; girders —
bone and vein — wait to impose
on the prone earth concrete
realities, scaffoldings
to correct our vision.

For a while pure idea
may hold its own, suspended,
framing the winter oaks, once tall,
in new dimensions.
But will then clashing
iron, stone, concrete and gnarled bough,
usurping geometries,
reinforce the landscape or destroy
delicate balances held in the water's flow?
These slow, unwieldy labours, can they blend
ever, grow human as the pliant trees
the grids begin to hide?

The willows big with leaf
blur outlines; the unrooted
building's scant embodiment
of glass flows like the river
through shifts of April light,
takes in the sunlit trees,
oak, willow, — a man too
is taken in, involved, watching
the landscape grow, sees his own
image, mirrored, blend and fade
with the sun.
                    For a while
all is one world,
new possibility.

But in season the winter spate
will bear away the rusted skeleton
leaf and ruins reassume
the land, earth have the last word.

The target they aim at lies in wait for them,
innocent as a bleached skull.
Astride their Nortons the council boys
skid here across dark skylines, blindly drawn
by the maelstrom of headlamps, their nostrils scenting
night shot through with daggers of light and music.
Leathered in black and appetites stropped keen,
they strut into clearings of light, the cool commanders.
Rain
dribbles, blistering the cinema hoardings'
ten-foot-high smiling faces
like acid.

Somnambulant, helmetted, like divers they glide
across bars, dance hall floors, exploring another element,
or loll round their girls, restless automata,
while wurlitzers pump out non-stop rainbow music.
Along the nude streets they parade their reluctant
innocence, but find

nothing that will resist or fight against
the heel's urgent thrust, the back-kicking pedal,
until in doorways, anywhere that's dry,
doubt is stifled in flesh. From such raw hulks
of buildings, words, a cry even, pain,
can force no resonance. Bland facades
baffle every sound but the engine's roar
till the only life
seems fast and away, a gaudy delirium
of wheels. This city holds
nothing that can pace their moods or offer
more than a vagrant tenderness shaken and split,
no promise more enduring
than the glory of petrol stains
rainbowed on wet asphalt, here, tonight.

Hotel Rooms

A non-entity, nothing to offend
Beyond its four walls and non-commital stucco;
Whatever tragic parting once took place
Within this bed, no secret tears have stained
The discreet drabness of the curtains, the decor
Survives each embrace, remains anonymous.

Only a playbill or a railway ticket
Left screwed up in the ashtray
Destroys their immunity, offers tantalizing
Clues to my predecessors as, in the early hours,
Lying awake, I hear the floorboards creaking,
The next room's door opened and quietly locked.

Next morning, with sheets at half-mast hung to air,
The room expands into the summer landscape; the
        guests
Have already left for their separate destinations,
The wardrobe bare, suitcases packed.
                Where ghostly hands caressed
Blundering human flesh, clean linen is turned, intact,
Chemically free of nostalgia, the finger prints removed
From the scene of the crime and hoovers swiftly applied
Where a sudden breeze through the doyleys has signed
        the dust.

Display Window

In full view of the fashionable shoppers
A sleek young man on padded feet assaults
The tailor's dummies behind plate glass. Perfunctorily
Flowered hat, veil and fifty-guinea coat
Slip from the model's elegant shoulders, revealing
Unnippled naked breasts, smooth thighs of plaster.
Finally even the wig goes. Yet these practised girls
Shrug off their humiliation, hands still beckon and wave
Invisible umbrellas or toy with prancing poodles. Though
Bald now and blatantly sexless, they retain their poise.
The furry customers shudder and pass on.

Bullfight

Enter
the knights, their horses padded,
blinkered, to parade
twice through the arena's golden
dust, until
to drumrolls, fanfares, banners
streaming, the bull
erupts from his black hold
into the muscled silence.

Amazed at first
by so much blaring light
closing in on him, he stands
his ground, tousled clenched head
butting, rounds on these men,
uncomprehending, as they stake
their brute knowledge against his
brute force, thrust out to be our kill.

With savage artistry the bandilleras
strike home, if silk flanks shot with blood,
glazed eye, hooves pawing for onslaught,
are home, the occupant so clearly
elsewhere.
                    He turns, gains speed,
blundering past as anger
shakes him, and the crowd cheers,
defaced by the late sunlight.
A good bull! They close. Feinting
an elegant twitch of hips
and calves, firm as a dancer's,
the matador. Inches too late
the bull stumbles past
his gleaming adversary.

For ten minutes, thronged by cheers,
our silken dandy

47

taunts him, wears him down,
prepares him for the final act, the great
initiation when, high priest,
to crowds straining forward, he holds
the sword in the red cape poised
for the coup de grace; like a crucifix
with artistic savagery the blade
plunges down over the horns,
between the shoulders, lethal,
lancing the heart, swift,
damnably graceful.

This other that we down,
our own darkness embodied, is slowly
crumbled onto his knees,
not suppliant, prostrate.
His foamed tongue swabs the dust.
The obstinate vast head
lifts once then like a broken
sunflower droops, slowly in blood
succumbs.

Nothing could be more dead,
ten minutes back a lashing thong
of fury,
this black, shabby bulk dragged off by mules.
Watching, we sacrifice the human heart.

A Miniature

All summer's nocturnal visitors, the moths
That galaxied our ceiling with wings of dust,
Rub out to powder, resign to the scavenging ants
More breath than substance.
                    Shards of heraldic beetles,
Cheated by muslin nets; wreckage of scorpions,
Caught lurking in corners and killed outright,
Their outstretched claws still malevolent; wasps cut in two;
A frantic spider drowning in the sink,
And squadrons of greasy flies
That suck in unseen worlds of pestilence:
All go berserk in their death throes, aeroplane engines
Revving before the take-off.

The ragged alleys and stairways are draped in sunlight,
Defiled by shadow. All the way up from the banks of the
    heavy Douro
The beggar children, the legless, the half-blind shout for
    escudos.

Over-exposed, says the tourist who, disbelieving
Stark black, stark white, abandons his camera, afraid to
    probe
Behind the whitewashed tenements into the wounds of
    darkness.

Here though the church retains her sanctuary, her relics;
Inside, an antique darkness offers relief,
Incense to drown the stench of poverty.

In the faint drone of voices old women grovel,
Half-buried in shawls and prayers. Here are true signs of
    healing,
An ear, a leg, a breast hanging in wax at the altar.

Outside by her granite base, foursquare on rock,
Picturesque hovels swarm, maggots around a carcase,
And experienced travellers discuss
Its magnificent position.

Shadows

A quietude of closed doors and shuttered air
Infests the countryside for miles around
With the fatigue of death; in this backwater
Of faded light the woods are thick with sound.

Winter descends, the scarecrow trees are felled,
Dead leaves lie down like matting on the path.
Untidily in ornamental pots
Dead flowers await the verger's day of wrath.

Stooping women addicted to this gloom
Fondle like relics flowers they have brought to dress
The altar's austerity with signs of home,
Accustomed now to their mortal loneliness.

Outsiders patiently salvage what they can,
Admire the lych-gate or the saxon font.
In search of light, they find the carved oak doors
Open on darkness, obscure and resonant.

Air rots the banners: woodworms, like consciences,
Interrogate the crumbling pews and weave
Through ornate carvings blurred by the spider's slang.
Filigree cobwebs drape the musty nave.

Art for death's sake, a place for the slowly dying
That rebukes all noise, keeps strangers at their distance.
Where low stone walls confine the wombs of earth
The scaffold trees adopt a chastened stance.

Dusk's the best time to visit here while still
An inkling of lichened light engraves the view
And sickly glints of stained-glass colour spill
Onto the waiting graves, cross-hatched with yew.

Virtues composed two hundred years ago
Are fenced around with privet and Gothic grills,
Their names erased by the wind and turned to dust,
Their owners compost for the daffodils.

Night battens down the antique countryside,
Distilling from each shade its private grief
Traced out in marble. The trusting dead relax
And hibernate until the tree sprouts leaf.

Snowfall

What I admire is
its wholly other syntax, the way
gulls' wings wheeling through smokelight,
ships' horns from unseen quays,
are loosed from their slurred, usual patterns, and
submerge into the silence, accepting
as if in amnesia the snow's
mute absolution.

This reformation zest,
whitewashing, creates
new images from calm, stirs latent
intensities of spirit;
snow, subtle iconoclast,
blurs stucco colonnades,
blunts the baroque statues,
and in their place with each
fresh onslaught distinguishes
in the everyday, jaded streets
a nuance of dogmatic whiteness,
elects the commonplace
to martyrdom, till the world
verges on incandescence.

Such purity, thank God,
such icy perfection,
cannot long survive
or it would spoil us.
The drifting winds subside,
hedges and trees retract
their unrelenting logic,
their white fruit falls, the skyline
reclines in grey. Next morning,
our saintly warders gone, we crush underfoot
a soiled vision, choosing instead
a mundane truth, shovelling
yesterday's wonder aside and glad to be merely human.

The Meeting

Winter. A bare room, silent,
smelling of floor polish.
A ring of good, scrubbed faces
who try not to see the grey
light outside burden
the frozen river nor hear
inside the radiator's
belching, groaning,
but, eyes clamped tight, direct
radar beams inwards,
scanning soul's outer space
for objects that may be
God, could emit
messages.
The silence drifts like snow.

Dazed then they return
to earth, the walls of broken
white again close in.
Where can their eyes rest?
No idols here save man
himself that might deflect
light from the plain glass
to focus his first sight
on merely human beauties.
(Yet in certain oblique
moments of sunlight even
simplest glass can prism
into a rainbow.)
The dove-grey silences
hold no annunciations.

Instead self-questionings pare
wasted flesh and blood
to its essential skeleton.
The mind's lens opens
only a split second, shutting

on a white silence, Siberias
of calm descend, till nothing
exists beyond the worn
carpet's pattern, the massive
simplicities that separate out
into black trees against
the white ground, negatives
of Spring's imagined landscapes.

And still no word has come.
If only we could know
this emptiness were all.
But where could the word alight
here? The clock on the landing
commands the room. Someone
on speaking terms with God
gets up to expound his love
or reason a way there.
But God's a two-way mirror:
attempt to penetrate that grey
and it is your own
distorted images stare back.
A flutter of words, then legs
uncross themselves, the interior
silence cracks like ice.
We rise, hands shake, we talk,
and for another week
let the inner darkness wait.

The Ballad of the Psycho-Analyst

They took me across the river,
they led me up the hill
and a white coat with a man inside
proclaimed me mentally ill.

"Don't fuss, my dear, don't worry,
we know what's best, you'll see.
You may have gone right out of your mind
but I have a skeleton key.

Don't smoke, don't drink, try not to think . . . "
When he left me he locked the door.
They have put me away for a rainy day
when my head won't hurt any more.

My wrist wears a disc with a number,
bright wires are tied to my head
and a balding angel in long, white robes
prescribes ten days in bed.

We chat about my childhood,
the colours I adored
and what I think when he says 'black ink'
or 'snake' or 'lake' or 'sword'.

My husband was ten years younger,
I married him for his looks.
"He became a thorn in my flesh," I said.
They wrote *that* down in their books.

They dredged and fathomed every dream
till through my waking they glowed
like luminous deep-sea fish
that when hauled to the surface explode.

I was once a manic depressive,
an arty blue-stocking, a beat,

but surgery cured me of culture
and set me back on my feet.

For they probed my skull with forceps
and removed a chunk of my brain
so that now I'm as well adjusted
as a ball is to a chain.

If you ask how I am, I'm fine:
I'm a demon for bingo and whist,
I'm a paid-up member of eighteen clubs,
I can swim, I can ski, I can ride, I can twist.
And I don't *imagine* things any more,
I'm a normal person again,
but in the recess that was once my soul
I still feel the absence of pain.

A Landscaped People

The silence exiled from cities
accumulates here, stowed
cloud-like behind mountains.

Snow-fences, telegraph poles and in summer
remote streamers of dust — these only
hint at a road, disturbing

the scrub, the wasted calm; sound
rarely travels so far. Hard country
but not hostile; indifferent,

just as it was taken and left
a hundred years back,
keeping man at his distance,

making him feel among
its wind-hung plateaus, overladen
with bluff, escarpment, spur,

nowhere at home for long.
Out of scale, an intruder,
he sets off above the tree-line

for more indulgent horizons
and finds the watershed, lakes
slowly collecting stillness

to replenish another
more distant ocean; red winds
prowling the dusk

and his hands calloused,
his face set west broken in furrows,
his jaw hewn with silence.

Raison d'être

Over low obstinate hills
planes steady, descend
to a chaos of lights —
streets, the railyard — jettisoned

a hundred years ago,
a trading post on the trek
west across the prairies:
now there's no going back,

the place exists, has a name,
and must continue, if only
for the real estate. Farmsteads
smothered in weeds waist-high

may die at the road's edge
but hardly a whole town
and not now those trees they planted
are avenues. It has all slowly grown

through depression and dusty summer, a place
without history, but a Pioneer Museum
on the main square and motels, drive-ins
lining the road out, a random

skyline of silos, feedgrain warehouses
and the Congregational Church, whose bulk at night
stands out against the surrounding darkness
of hushed corn, its cross neon-lit

till day, encased in lead, lowers it back
into the prairie. The town has learnt to wait.
Light planes hang like birds of prey,
buses flicker past on the Interstate,

and in time the nomad suburbs that stretch
miles beyond the original stockade, settle
in lieu of a gold rush or an airforce base
pro. tem. for mere survival.

Names

'Close to this point in 1542 . . . '
We park our air-conditioned Valiant,
walk to the historical marker, read:
(around us only the desert we'd travelled through
all morning at sixty, dry creeks, nothing to see)
— expense of spirit pulped to mere event.
Nuñez de Vaca, Vasquez de Coronado,
the land's founders, beautiful sounding names,
commanders for whom possession was
the sincerest form of flattery; but their rhetoric
in these sparse valleys shouted itself hoarse
and found no echo. Nor could their blood succour
a single desert flower. Nothing took root:
betrayed or dead of thirst after ten months exploring,
the expected spring dry, the reinforcements
diverted or lost, defamed, imprisoned, they died
five thousand miles from home.
The bone-white sand still trickles through our fingers:
'we cannot escape history'.

                              Conquistadors
shifted like cloud shadows across the mountains
through New Spain's precarious settlements.
Land, serfs, souls for God or gold for men
lured them past abandoned stockades, finally
to burden the ocean with the Aztec's golden skill,
spoils of empire, for Philip to melt down.
They pryed out the 'seven cities', found
villages of mud scooped from the rock face.
(we thought it would be quiet here and it is quiet,
not a motel for miles, no signs of civilization)
But the land became over-cultivated
and where long grasses flowered into dust
golden sand blooms beer cans, chunks of tyre.
The past is what we imagine.

The mission is concluded. At Mescalero
Apaches fortified by hooch don feathers
once a year and paleface tourists come
sporting sun-tan, transistors, to join in the war-dance.
But the serpent's skin is shrugged off, the headgear abandoned,
museums label their sticks and stones, tame behind glass.
And for the rest, the unsettled, ex-colonials
in Drake's Bay, San Antonio, Baton Rouge,
sandstorms deleted all trace
of their lost ancestors
and the reminding names hurt most of all.

Modus Vivendi

Brute at first light
the wagons' dereliction
unsoftened by sunflowers yellowing the track
as the express submerges and is sucked back
into terminal darkness.

Light they could not impose, the pioneers,
but took over, naturalized the darkness, and at last
tamed it to chiaroscuro: golden
reflections splinter and crash
in the rebuff of noon, overhead girders
shadow a convoy of trucks that sirens and lamps stampede
through brick canyons . . .

However far
the highways fan out ten lanes wide and always lead on,
however high the blind walls grope to catch
the sun, however bright
the sidewalks dizzy with neon,
there comes no further west, the continent dawn exposes
is trading in futures only: the squatters moving on
past the same clutter of hoardings, the same shacks,
leave behind them the skins of a civilization
not yet finally settled, and do not know
when they'll be coming back.

Through three thousand miles the granite night is blasted
by wheels' thunder and outlying suburbs hollowed
by the howl of a brute bearing away
their portable loneliness.

63